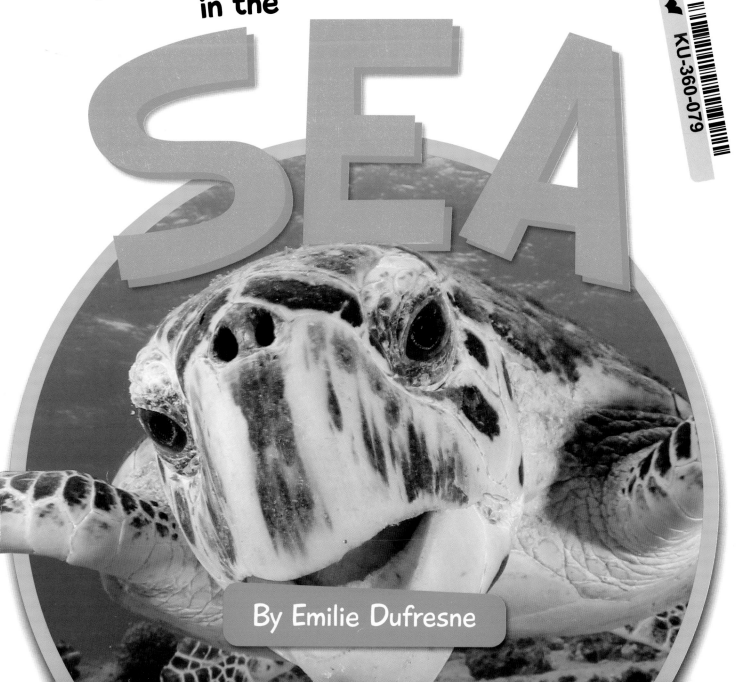

ENDANGERED ANIMALS
in the
SEA

By Emilie Dufresne

BookLife
PUBLISHING

©2021
BookLife Publishing Ltd.
King's Lynn
Norfolk PE30 4LS

All rights reserved.
Printed in Malta.

A catalogue record for
this book is available from
the British Library.

ISBN: 978-1-83927-465-7

Written by:
Emilie Dufresne

Edited by:
Madeline Tyler

Designed by:
Jasmine Pointer

PHOTO CREDITS

*All images are courtesy of Shutterstock.com, unless otherwise specified.
With thanks to Getty Images, Thinkstock Photo and iStockphoto. Cover –
Rich Carey, Damsea. 4–5 – Johannes Asslaber, In Green, Ethan Daniels,
Imagine Earth Photography. 6–7 – irin-k. 8–9 – lzoe, Yoshinori, Rich
Carey. 10–11 – Rich Carey, Vladimir Sviracevic, Kleber Cordeiro, Laverne
Nash. 12–13 – LuisMiguelEstevez, NarisaFotoSS, Ken Schulze. 14–15 –
Moira Brown and New England Aquarium / Attribution, Steve Meese,
KBel. 16–17 – Al McGlashan, SergeUWPhoto. 18–19 – jodyo.photos, ohrim,
Ryan M. Bolton, cdrin, VeronikaMaskova. 20–21 – New York Zoological
Society. / Public domain, John A. Anderson. 22–23 – Volodymyr Goinyk,
Shane Gross, wildestanimal, Brocreative, KLUSER, Jag_cz.*

CONTENTS

Page 4   Being Endangered

Page 6   A Closer Look at the Categories

Page 8   The Ocean Habitat

Page 10   Hawksbill Turtles

Page 12   Angelsharks

Page 14   North Atlantic Right Whales

Page 16   Southern Bluefin Tuna

Page 18   Sea Otters

Page 20   Now Extinct

Page 22   Success Stories

Page 23   Save the Animals

Page 24   Glossary and Index

Words that look like <u>this</u> can be found in the glossary on page 24.

ENDANGERED

When a <u>species</u> of animal is endangered, it means that it is in danger of going extinct. When a species is extinct, it means there are no more of that animal left alive in the world.

Red pandas are an endangered species.

There are lots of different reasons that a species might become endangered. For example, the <u>climate crisis</u> can change a species' <u>habitat</u> and make it hard for it to survive there.

Healthy coral reef

Dead coral reef

The climate crisis is making the oceans warmer.
The water is becoming too warm for many ocean animals.

A Closer Look at the
CATEGORIES

Different species are put into different categories depending on how <u>threatened</u> they are.

Data Deficient – Not enough information to know what category the species is in

Least Concern – Currently not in danger of going extinct

Near Threatened – Likely to be threatened soon

Vulnerable – Facing a high <u>risk</u> of extinction in the wild

Always check this website to find the most up-to-date information...

www.iucnredlist.org

Endangered – Facing a very high risk of extinction in the wild

Critically Endangered – Facing extremely high risk of extinction in the wild

Extinct in the Wild – When a species can no longer be found in the wild and only lives in <u>captivity</u>

Extinct – When a species no longer exists in the world

The OCEAN HABITAT

Oceans cover around seven-tenths of the Earth's surface. Ocean water is salty. Some parts of the ocean are deep and dark, and other parts are shallow and sandy.

Tiger shark

There are lots of different ocean habitats all over the world. The animals that live in them face many more challenges than the climate crisis, including <u>pollution</u> and hunting.

Plastic pollution in the ocean

HAWKSBILL TURTLES

One of the main threats facing hawksbill turtles is <u>poaching</u>. They are killed for their shells and meat.

Humans also eat their eggs, even though it is against the law to do so.

NAME:
Hawksbill turtle

FOUND:
Warm ocean waters

CATEGORY:
Critically endangered

Hawksbill turtles found

Some people <u>volunteer</u> to protect these turtles.

Hawksbill turtles lay their eggs on hot, sandy beaches. As people travel to these beaches more and more, it is harder for them to find places to lay their eggs.

ANGELSHARKS

• Angelsharks found

The shallow waters along beaches are often busy with people. This disturbs younger angelsharks that stay in sandy areas near to the coast.

NAME:
Angelshark

FOUND:
Sandy areas around
Europe and the
Mediterranean Sea

CATEGORY:
Critically endangered

Trawling net

Trawling catches, and
often kills, sea creatures
that aren't being fished
for, including angelsharks.

Angelsharks lie under the sand at the bottom of the sea.
This makes it easy for them to get caught up in trawling nets.
Trawling nets can be very big, and often drag along the seabed.

RIGHT WHALES

North Atlantic right whales can be hit and killed by big ships in the ocean.

NAME:
North Atlantic right whale

FOUND:
Across the North Atlantic Ocean

CATEGORY:
Critically endangered

North Atlantic right whales are also often caught in fishing nets. This can kill the whales and can leave many more with scars on them.

North Atlantic right whales found

Looking at the scars on the whales can help us to understand how often they are tangled and hit.

BLUEFIN TUNA

NAME:
Southern bluefin tuna

FOUND:
Warm waters in the south

CATEGORY:
Critically endangered

Southern bluefin tuna have been overfished for a long time. This means too many fish are caught and there is not enough time to replace them through <u>breeding</u>.

Lots of people <u>illegally</u> catch southern bluefin tuna because they can be sold for a lot of money.

Lots is being done to try and make sure these animals are fished <u>sustainably</u>.

• Southern bluefin tuna found

SEA OTTERS

The climate crisis is causing more storms in the sea otters' habitat. It is also making the water they live in more <u>acidic</u>.

NAME:
Sea otter

FOUND:
Coastal areas in North America and northern Asia

CATEGORY:
Endangered

These changes to the sea otters' habitat make it harder for them to survive there.

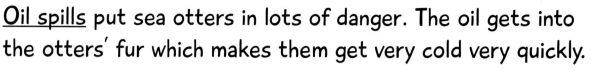

Oil spills put sea otters in lots of danger. The oil gets into the otters' fur which makes them get very cold very quickly.

Oil spill, Mauritius

Sea otters found

If the otters eat or breathe in the oil, they may not survive.

NOW EXTINCT

CARIBBEAN MONK SEAL

Caribbean monk seals are thought to have been extinct since 1952. They were hunted and killed for their blubber, or fat, which was used to light lamps and as cooking oil.

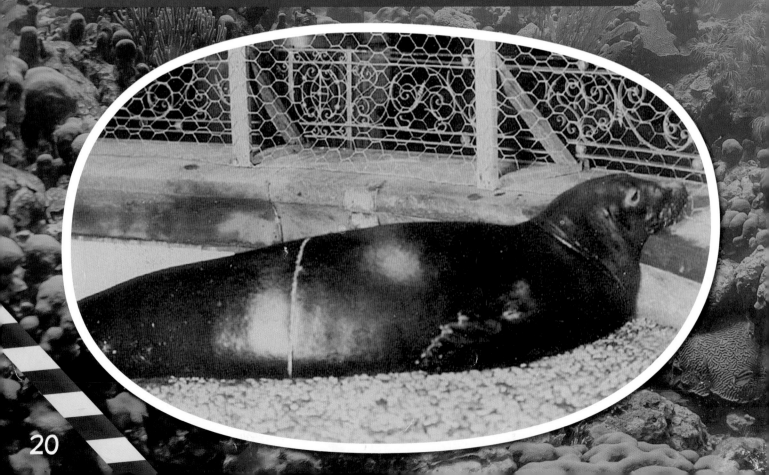

CORAL REEFS

Coral reefs are very important to the ocean habitat. They are home to many sea creatures and protect the coast from powerful waves. Many types of coral are in danger of going extinct.

The climate crisis, pollution and fishing are threatening coral reefs across the world.

SUCCESS STORIES

Humpback whales were nearly extinct, but now they are 'least concern'.

The Ocean Cleanup project has started removing plastic and rubbish from the sea.

The coral reefs that we do have left are being protected by different charities and scientists.

SAVE the ANIMALS!

How can you help endangered sea creatures around the world?

Be an eco-tourist and make sure that where you go and what you do on holiday isn't harming the animals and habitat around you.

Try to eat less fish. If you do eat fish, ask an adult to make sure it was caught sustainably.

SUSTAINABLE FISHING ✓

GLOSSARY

acidic — contains something that causes damage to some plants and animals

breeding — when two animals create young together

captivity — kept in a zoo or safari park and not in the wild

climate crisis — the very serious problems that are being caused by human action and the changes these actions make in the natural world

habitat — the natural home in which animals, plants and other living things live

illegally — to do something that is against the law

oil spills — when oil is spilt into water and floats on top of it

poaching — to illegally hunt and kill an animal

pollution — harmful or dirty things that are put into nature by humans

risk — when there is a chance that something might happen

species — a group of very similar animals or plants that can create young together

sustainably — doing something in a way that doesn't cause harm and can be continued

threatened — not sure of whether a type of animal or plant will survive

volunteer — giving your time for free to help others

INDEX

Atlantic Ocean 14—15

coasts 12, 18, 21

coral reefs 5, 21—22

eggs 10—11

fishing 13, 15—17, 21, 23

nets 13, 15

oil 19—20

sand 8, 11—13

ships 14